WITH YOU, DEAR CHILD, IN MIND

Lynn Groth

Copyright 1985 by the Board for Parish Education
Wisconsin Ev. Lutheran Synod
Milwaukee, Wisconsin 53222
All rights reserved. Printed in U.S.A.

ISBN 0-938272-77-2

He came to earth with you in mind,
That Baby, oh, so small.

His name is Jesus, God's own Son.
He came to die for all.

When Jesus grew to be a boy
He loved to hear God's Word.
He knew He came to earth to be
Our Savior and our Lord.

Jesus always did obey
What Mary and Joseph said.
Never once did evil thoughts
Come into Jesus' head.

As a man, the Savior did
Things only God can do.
He healed the sick, made water wine;
Fed hungry people, too.

He showed His power as God's own Son
By bringing back the dead.
He told one dead young girl to rise.
She got right out of bed!

But many people did not trust
In Jesus and His Word.
Some had an evil plan in mind:
To kill our precious Lord.

They took Him as their prisoner;
They hardly had to try,
For Jesus walked right up to them.
He knew He had to die.

That was the only way to save
The world from sin, you see.
Only God's own perfect Son
Could die for you and me.

They nailed the Savior to a cross.
He hung there all the day.
And when He gave His life for us,
He for our sins did pay.

He died for us on Friday;
   Was put into a grave.
Some soldiers came to watch the tomb.
   They stood there, tall and brave.

But Sunday morn they shook with fear,
  For an angel, white as snow
Suddenly appeared to them;
  An empty grave to show.

The Savior was not in the tomb.
He was no longer dead.
"The Savior is alive again!"
The Easter angel said.

Jesus truly was alive.
He'd risen from the dead.
A few more days He spent on earth
To tell what God's Word said.

Then to His followers He said,
"Tell others of My love."
And then He rose into the sky;
Back to His home above.

Jesus lived and died and rose
With you, dear child, in mind.

He wants you to believe in Him—
The Savior, good and kind.

Yes, Jesus still has you in mind.
He cares for you each day.

He's always with you, at your side;

At work, at rest, at play.

And someday you will be with Him
In heaven up above.

He has a home there just for you.
How great is Jesus' love!

A prayer for you to say:

Oh, thank You, precious Savior!
I love You, Lord and King.
Please help me always trust in You.
To You alone I sing!
　　　Amen.